# The Principal Navies Of The World In 1898

## Naval Constructor Sussenguth

In the interest of creating a more extensive selection of rare historical book reprints, we have chosen to reproduce this title even though it may possibly have occasional imperfections such as missing and blurred pages, missing text, poor pictures, markings, dark backgrounds and other reproduction issues beyond our control. Because this work is culturally important, we have made it available as a part of our commitment to protecting, preserving and promoting the world's literature. Thank you for your understanding.

OFFICE OF NAVAL INTELLIGENCE.

PART I: GENERAL INFORMATION SERIES, No. XVIII.

INFORMATION FROM ABROAD.

# NOTES

ON

# NAVAL PROGRESS.

APRIL, 1899.

OFFICE OF NAVAL INTELLIGENCE.

———•◆•———

WASHINGTON:
GOVERNMENT PRINTING OFFICE.
1899.

~~H.2662.10~~
War 7108.99

From the
U. S. Government.

# THE PRINCIPAL NAVIES OF THE WORLD IN 1898.

BY

NAVAL CONSTRUCTOR SÜSSENGUTH,
IMPERIAL GERMAN NAVY.

TRANSLATED FROM THE GERMAN.

# INTRODUCTORY.

An article by Naval Constructor Süssenguth, German Navy, published in the March number of the Marine-Rundschau, issued at Berlin, giving a comparison of the principal navies of the world in 1898, has been found concise and instructive, and is given in this the first of the General Information Series for 1899. The difficulty of obtaining exact information regarding vessels of other nations will be apparent from errors regarding our own Navy in this seemingly carefully prepared article, some of which are corrected in footnotes by this office.

RICHARDSON CLOVER,
*Commander, U. S. N., Chief Intelligence Officer.*

NAVY DEPARTMENT, *April 29, 1899.*

Approved:
A. S. CROWNINSHIELD,
*Rear-Admiral, U. S. N., Chief of Bureau of Navigation.*

# THE PRINCIPAL NAVIES OF THE WORLD IN 1898.

By Naval Constructor SÜSSENGUTH, *Imperial German Navy.*

[Translated from the Marine Rundschau, March, 1899.]

The unusual development of traffic and navigation during the last ten years, the tendency toward expansion of colonial possessions, and other reasons have caused in almost all countries a greater expenditure for the increase and maintenance of navies.

The following table will give an idea of the naval budgets of the different powers:

*Expenses in million marks.*

|  | 1897. | | 1898. | | 1899. | | Estimates proposed or granted for new constructions and armaments. | |
| --- | --- | --- | --- | --- | --- | --- | --- | --- |
|  | Total budget. | For new constructions and armaments. | Total budget. | For new constructions and armaments. | Total budget. | For new constructions and armaments. | Total. | For one year. |
| England | 450 | 250 | [1] 580 | [1] 370 |  | [1] 370 |  | [1] 370 |
| France | 202 | 94 | 230 | 121 | 250 |  | 300 | [1] 180 |
| Russia | 223 | 74 | 260 | 121 |  | 55 | 482 | [1] 60 |
| Germany | 118 | 49 | 122 | 51.4 |  | 55 | 482 | [1] 60 |
| United States | 138 | 55 | 338 | 219 | 224 | 105 |  | [1] 200 |
| Japan | 147 | 128 | 180 | 150 | 200 | 160 | [1] 400 | [1] 70 |
| Italy | 82 | 37 | 82 | 44 |  | [1] 80 | 240 | [1] 80 |
| Austria | 23 | 6 | 25 | 6 | 28 | 15 | 90 | [1] 27 |

[1] Approximately.

It will be seen from the last column that, although there is a general idea prevailing that particularly high demands have been made in Germany on the taxing capacity of the country, this is not the case, and that the annual amount of our budget for new constructions does not even reach the amount required for the same purpose in Italy during the next few years, although our merchant marine is three times as large as that of the latter country.

Relative to the cost of modern battleships in different countries, the chief constructor of the English navy publishes some figures according to which the English battleships *Nile* and *Trafalgar*, 1885, cost 17,000,000 marks each, while those of the *Royal Sovereign* class cost something less, and those of the *Majestic* type something more. The cost of the *Powerful* was 13,600,000 marks. These figures indicate the cost of construction exclusive of armament and ammunition. The new French battleships cost 20,000,000 marks each, the United States *Indiana* 18,800,000, and the latest German battleships 14,000,000 marks. By figuring the price per ton for the purpose of comparison, using that of the *Majestic* as a base, and calling it 1, the *Nile* costs 1.28 per ton, the French battleships 1.39, the *Indiana* 1.42, and the *Kaiser Friedrich Wilhelm* only 1.06 per ton. If we take into consideration that the last-named ship has been equipped with the new Krupp armor, which costs about one-fifth more than the armor employed on the *Majestic*, it will be seen that Germany is able to build her warships as cheaply or even more cheaply than England, which, in view of the very recent beginnings of German naval construction, must be considered an excellent result. In France the high cost of ships for war and commercial purposes appears to be due to the sluggish working of the administration. As to Russia, Sir William White was unable to give figures, but it is his opinion that they will be very high as regards the new Russian cruisers.

The number of new ships to be constructed is in harmony with the increased budgets of the different powers. The following table will show the status of the different navies according to a report issued by the British Parliament in July, 1898:

|  | Completed. | | | | | | | Under construction. | | | | | | |
| --- | --- | --- | --- | --- | --- | --- | --- | --- | --- | --- | --- | --- | --- | --- |
|  | England. | France. | Russia. | Germany. | Italy. | United States. | Japan. | England. | France. | Russia. | Germany. | Italy. | United States. | Japan. |
| Battleships | 52 | 27 | 12 | 9 | 15 | 5 | 3 | 12 | 8 | 6 | 5 | 2 | 8 | 3 |
| Armored cruisers | 18 | 9 | 10 | 3 | 3 | 2 | 1 | 8 | 10 | 1 | 2 | 2 | .... | 6 |
| Protected cruisers | 95 | 30 | 3 | 7 | 15 | 14 | 10 | 24 | 10 | 3 | 8 | 3 | 1 | 6 |
| Unprotected cruisers | 16 | 16 | 3 | 21 | 1 | 10 | 8 | .... | .... | .... | .... | .... | .... | 1 |
| Coast-defense ships | 15 | 14 | 15 | 19 | .... | [1]20 | 3 | .... | .... | 1 | .... | .... | .... | .... |
| Torpedo vessels | 35 | 13 | 17 | 2 | 15 | .... | 1 | .... | 2 | .... | .... | .... | .... | .... |
| Ships for special purposes | 3 | 1 | 5 | 1 | 2 | 1 | .... | .... | .... | .... | .... | .... | .... | .... |
| Torpedo-boat destroyers | 50 | .... | 1 | .... | .... | .... | .... | 46 | 8 | 28 | 1 | 1 | 20 | 8 |
| Torpedo boats | 98 | 211 | 114 | 113 | 142 | [2]8 | 44 | .... | 38 | .... | 9 | 2 | 22 | 12 |

[1] Including 6 double-turret monitors, 13 old single-turret monitors, and the ram Katahdin. The 13 old monitors would hardly be included in computing the strength of the Navy on the usual basis of age, speed, etc.—(O. N. I.)

[2] Torpedo boats completed, 13; under construction, 13.—(O. N. I.)

The above table shows that Japan is the only country building unprotected cruisers at the present time. Hence, it appears to be the intention of all the other nations to be represented abroad only by protected and efficient cruisers, especially since the battles of the Yalu and of Cavite and Santiago have removed the last doubt as to the worthlessness of unprotected ships in battle. The reason why coast-defense vessels are no longer being built except in Russia may be sought in the tendency of the powers to construct in their place only such ships as are adapted for battle on the open sea, viz, battleships. As a general thing, the question as to whether two small vessels would not be preferable in a battle to one ship twice as large has everywhere been decided in favor of the one large ship. All countries are at present building battleships of about 12,000 tons, England and Japan even of 15,000 tons, which latter displacement, as far as now known, is also contemplated for the new battleships to be commenced in France during the present year. The results of the battles of the Yalu and Santiago have shown the wisdom of such action. At the Yalu, the two Chinese battleships, which in offensive and defensive power were superior to the Japanese armored cruisers, were not put out of action, although the Japanese were at a great advantage by reason of the large number of their ships that were still in fighting condition at the end of the battle. At Santiago, the large American battleships soon brought about the destruction of the Spanish ships. Another circumstance in favor of the employment of large ships is the difficulty of providing the requisite trained complements for all the ships. A large ship does not require as large a crew as two vessels half the size. If, nevertheless, some of the powers are building smaller battleships, it may be safely assumed that the reason is lack of funds or that the ships in question are intended for limited modes of warfare.

## ENGLAND.

The value of the English navy, which in 1887 amounted to 740,000,000 marks, has now risen to 1,944,000,000 marks, exclusive of torpedo boats. The total displacement is 955,000 tons, and will reach 1,000,000 tons in the course of the next year. The total horsepower of all the ships' engines, again exclusive of torpedo boats, amounts to 1,575,000 tons.

The budget allowed for 1898-99 amounts to about 480,000,000 marks. Hence it exceeds that of the previous year by only about 30,000,000. The small increase is due, first of all, to the fact that, by reason of the great strikes among metal workers in England, the credits of the preceding year were not exhausted. The construction of the first-class battleships *Cæsar*, *Illustrious*, and *Hannibal*, for instance, has been so retarded that they could not begin their trial trips until the present year. The construction of the *Diadem* also has been delayed. As a further reason, it is stated that the 30.5-centimeter and 15-centimeter guns for the new ships had to be tested and remodeled to suit modern requirements; moreover, that the armor-plate factories were behind with their orders, owing to experiments with the new hardening process (Krupp process). It is also stated in the budget report that the plans of the four new battleships heretofore granted—the *Vengeance* (*Canopus* type), *Implacable*, *Irresistible*, and *Formidable*—had been completed and the ships given out for construction. Three new battleships are asked for (now named the *London*, *Venerable*, and *Bulwark*), which, with slight deviations, are to follow the *Formidable* type—length, 121.9 meters; beam, 22.8 meters; mean draft, 8.15 meters; displacement, 14,900 tons; I. H. P., 15,000; the armament consists of four 30.5-centimeter, twelve 15-centimeter, and thirty small R. F. guns; also four armored cruisers—the *Cressy*, *Aboukir*, *Hogue*, and *Sutlej*—and four sloops. The intention was to have under construction or engaged in trial trips during the past year 12 battleships, 16 first-class cruisers, 6 second-class cruisers, 16 third-class cruisers, 6 sloops, 4 twin-screw gunboats, 41 torpedo-boat destroyers, and 1 royal yacht.

Of other items of the budget we will mention the appropriation of the necessary funds for the acquisition of 200 new Whitehead torpedoes to take the place of 300 antiquated torpedoes that have been condemned; also the introduction of the Lee-Metford rifle.

Now that the program of naval constructions submitted by the Government has been allowed, the English navy should feel strong enough to be able to meet with decided superiority the combined fleets of any two adversaries. Shortly after the approval of the program it became known that the Czar had allowed the sum of 300,000,000 marks, to be distributed over three or four years, for the increase of the Russian fleet, in addition to the regular budget for new constructions. This report produced considerable excitement in England and caused the British Admiralty to submit to Parliament in July last a supplement to the naval estimates. The result was that in England also 300,000,000 marks, to be distributed over three years, were voted by a large majority, which shows how easily the English are aroused at the slightest menace to their naval supremacy and how well the nation has been trained to understand the importance of protecting its commerce and colonies.

The following table gives an idea of the floating material now under construction and to be completed within three years at the latest, which alone is superior in power to the total German navy as it will be constituted at the completion of the naval programme in 1903:[1]

|  | Already launched. | Under construction. | Not yet begun. |
|---|---|---|---|
| Battleships | 4 | 5 | 7 |
| Armored cruisers and first-class cruisers | 4 | 7 | 6 |
| Second-class cruisers | 5 | 1 | |
| Third-class cruisers | 7 | | |
| Gunboats | | 4 | 4 |

Exclusive of all ships and torpedo-boat destroyers already turned over for the purpose of trial trips.

In connection with the battleships, it should be noted that the four already launched and two of the ships under construction belong to

---

[1] This comparison is true of the United States Navy, as well as of the German. The increase in tonnage to be added to the British Navy within the next three years exceeds the total tonnage of the war vessels of the United States Navy, built and building, by more than 100,000 tons displacement.—(O. N. I.)

## FIG. 1.

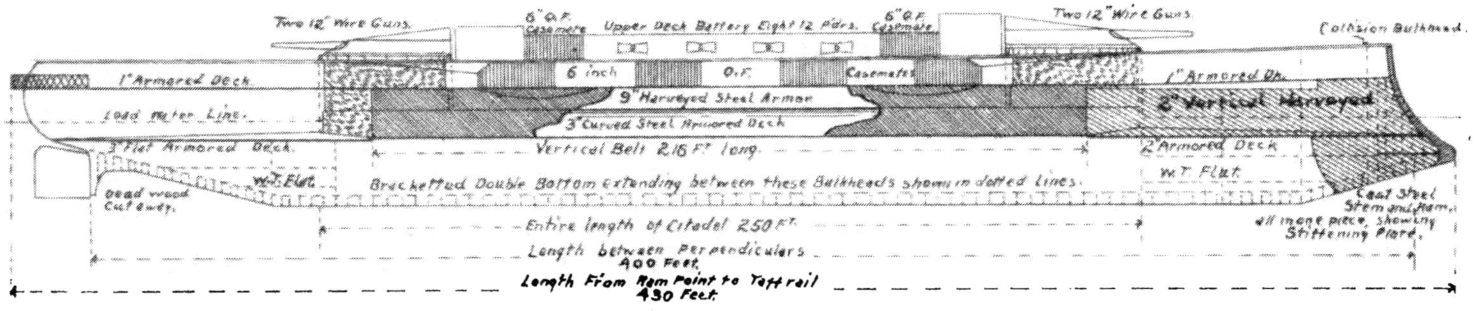

"FORMIDABLE."
SKETCH OF ARMOR.

the *Canopus* class, of 12,950 tons displacement and 18.25 knots speed. These ships are sufficiently well known, and we will only show in a sketch how the forward part of the ship is to be armored, this being the first instance where England has extended the armor to the stem.

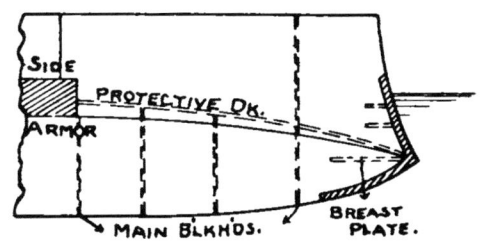

FIG. 2.
"FORW'D PART OF RESOLUTION."

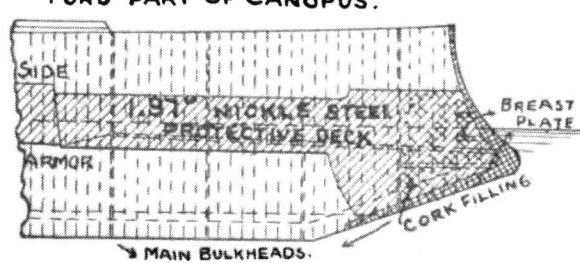

FIG. 3.
"FORD PART OF CANOPUS."

From the above sketch it will appear that the armor of these battleships is similar to that in use in Germany, Austria, and the United States, except that the thickness of the armor belt is only 50 millimeters, so that even small-caliber R. F. guns could pierce it. The unprotectedness of the extremities of English battleships is the subject of animated discussion in France, the opinion being that by the use of French melinite shells the outer skin forward and aft of the citadel could be completely destroyed, and this would permit the water to enter the protective deck and materially impair the manœuvering efficiency of the ship. On the other hand, the English think that a hit under the French barbette turret would cause its collapse.

The other three battleships under construction, and three of those not yet commenced, are to belong to one and the same type. They are the *Formidable, Implacable, Irresistible, London, Venerable,* and *Bulwark,* of 15,000 tons displacement and 18 knots speed. They are to receive even more extensive armor protection than the *Canopus* class, but in the installation of guns and other respects they are to be similar. The battleships not yet given out for construction are to receive less armor protection than the *Formidable* class, but greater speed and less draught, so as to enable them to pass through the Suez Canal.

From the above it is evident that all of the thirty-three first-class English battleships built during the last few years, or about to be built, belong to one and the same type, differing only in minor details, so that they can all be used for the same purpose and combined into squadrons in any manner desired.

The four cruisers already launched, and one of those under construction, belong to the *Diadem* class. The other four under construction, and two of those not yet begun, are the armored cruisers *Cressy*, *Aboukir*, *Hogue*, *Sutley*, *Bacchante*, and *Mutine*.

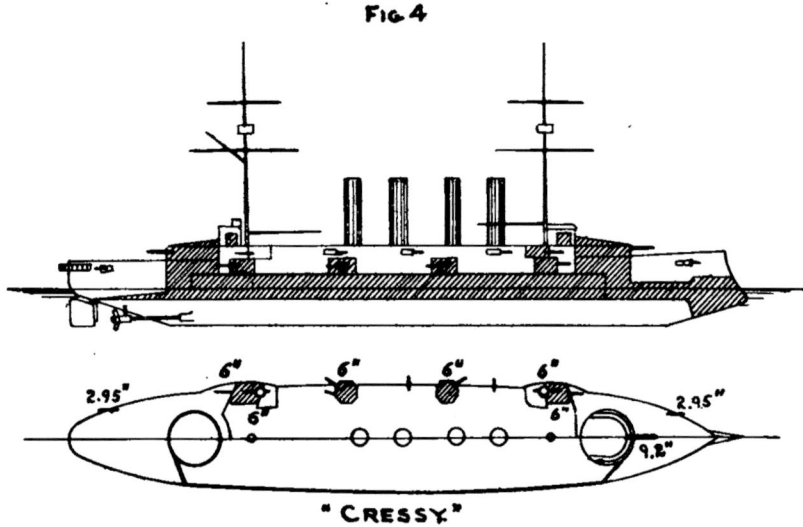

Fig 4

"CRESSY"

As England has built no armored cruisers since 1886, when the rather unsatisfactory *Aurora* class was completed, it is somewhat startling that six armored cruisers should be included in this year's program; but when it is remembered that all of the large cruisers built by France during the last few years have been armored cruisers, and that six of these, with a displacement of 9,515 tons each, were laid down during the past year, this significant step on the part of the English Admiralty will be readily understood.

Moreover, it is the endeavor in England to build a type having all the characteristics of armored cruisers—speed, radius of action, etc., and being at the same time adapted to fight in squadron formation by the side of the new English battleships. The new *Cressy* class might be designated as a modification of the *Canopus* type. The weight gained by the decrease of the armament has been utilized for increassing the engine power and radius of action. The distribution of the medium artillery, the protection of the ship's hull and of the guns is the same. The dimensions are: length, 134 meters; beam, 21 meters; draught, 7.9 meters; displacement, 12,000 tons. With this displacement, the coal supply is only 800 tons; but the total capacity of the coal bunkers is 2,000 tons, in which case the displacement would be increased to 13,200 tons. In order to attain a speed of 21 knots, which is 3 knots in excess of that of the English battleships, the length had to be increased by about 14 meters, requiring 21,000 I. H. P. For other particulars as to armor and armament see figs. 3 and 4.

Two others of the cruisers not yet commenced are also to be armored cruisers, but of dimensions differing from those of the *Cressy* class. They are to be giants, like the *Powerful* and *Terrible*, of 151 meters length, 21.5 meters beam, 7.9 meters draught, 14,100 tons displacement, 1,250 tons coal supply, and 30,000 I. H. P. With all bunkers filled, the ships will be able to carry 2,500 tons of coal, raising the displacement to 15,350 tons. From Lord Goschen's speech on the budget it would appear that these two ships are to be built in order that the English navy may be able to oppose to the six new French armored cruisers, *Montcalm*, etc., and to the *Jeanne d'Arc*, an adversary superior in every respect. This is the same policy that England adopted when she constructed the *Powerful* and *Terrible*, the largest protected cruisers hitherto built, as an offset for the new American commerce-destroyers *Columbia* and *Minneapolis* and the Russian *Rurik*. These two cruisers were to prove last year whether they answered the purpose for which they were built; but so far they have not come up to expectations.

The total tonnage of all English cruisers under construction is greater than that of the cruisers contemplated or under construction of all other European powers together.

The river gunboats built for service on the Nile are quite remarkable. They are being transported by rail in eleven separate parts, each capable of floating by itself to above the cataracts of the Nile, where they will again be put together.

The following table gives the principal dimensions of all English ships under construction or completed during the past year:

[NOTE.—Sub. l. t. = submerged launching-tubes; a. w. l. t. = above-water launching-tubes; R. F. = rapid-fire guns.]

| Name of type-ship. | Pelorus. | Arrogant. | Hermes. | Diadem. | Cressy. | Powerful. | New large cruisers. | Majestic. | Canopus. | Formidable. |
|---|---|---|---|---|---|---|---|---|---|---|
| Number ships of type | 11 | 4 | 3 | 8 | 6 | 2 | 2 | 9 | 6 | 6 |
| Length ........ meters | 91.4 | 97.5 | 108.7 | 132.6 | 134.1 | 152.4 | 151 | 119 | 118.8 | 121.9 |
| Beam .......... do | 11.12 | 17.48 | 16.5 | 21.0 | 21.2 | 21.6 | 21.5 | 23 | 22.5 | 22.8 |
| Draught ....... do | 4.11 | 7.16 | 6.4 | 7.7 | 7.9 | 8.2 | 7.9 | 8.6 | 7.9 | 8.15 |
| Displacement .. tons | 2,135 | 5,810 | 5,600 | 11,000 | 12,000 | 14,200 | 14,100 | 14,900 | 12,950 | 14,900 |
| Speed ......... knots | 20.7 | 19.6 | 19.5 | 20.75 | 21 | 22 | 23 | 17.5 | 18.25 | 18.5 |
| Horsepower | 7,028 | 10,290 | 10,000 | 18,000 | 21,000 | 25,000 | 30,000 | 11,000 | 13,500 | 15,000 |
| Armor belt .... millimeters | | | | 152.4 | 152.4 | 152.4 | 152.4 | 228 | 152 | 228 |
| Casemate ...... do | | | | 152.4 | 152.4 | 152.4 | 152.4 | 150 | 152 | (?) |
| Deck armor .... do | 51 | 51 | 75-34 | 102-64 | 76-51 | 152-76 | (?) | 100-63 | 63 | 101-63 |
| Armament | 8 10-cm. | 4 15-cm. | 11 12-cm. | 16 15-cm. | 2 23.3-cm. | 2 23.3-cm. | 2 23-cm. | 4 30.5-cm. | 4 30.5-cm. | 4 30.5-cm. |
| | 8 4.7-cm. | 6 12-cm. | 8 R.F. | 17 R.F. | 12 15-cm. | 12 15-cm. | 16 R.F. | 12 15-cm. | 12 15-cm. | 12 15-cm. |
| | 2 l.t. | 8 7.5-cm. | 2 sub.l.t. | 2 sub.l.t. | 17 R.F. | 30 R.F. | (?) | 16 7.5-cm. | 12 7.5-cm. | 16 7.5-cm. |
| | | 2 sub.l.t. | | | 2 sub.l.t. | 2 sub.l.t. | | 12 4.7-cm. | 6 4.7-cm. | 12 4.7-cm. |
| | | | | | | | | 1 a.w.l.t. | 4 sub.l.t. | 1 a.w.l.t. |
| | | | | | | | | 4 sub.l.t. | | 4 sub.l.t. |
| Coal supply .... tons | 250 | 1,175 | 550–1,050 | 1,000–2,000 | 800–2,000 | 1,500–2,500 | 1,250–2,500 | 900–2,250 | 1,900 | (?) |
| Complement | 224 | 419 | 450 | (?) | (?) | 900 | (?) | (?) | 750 | (?) |

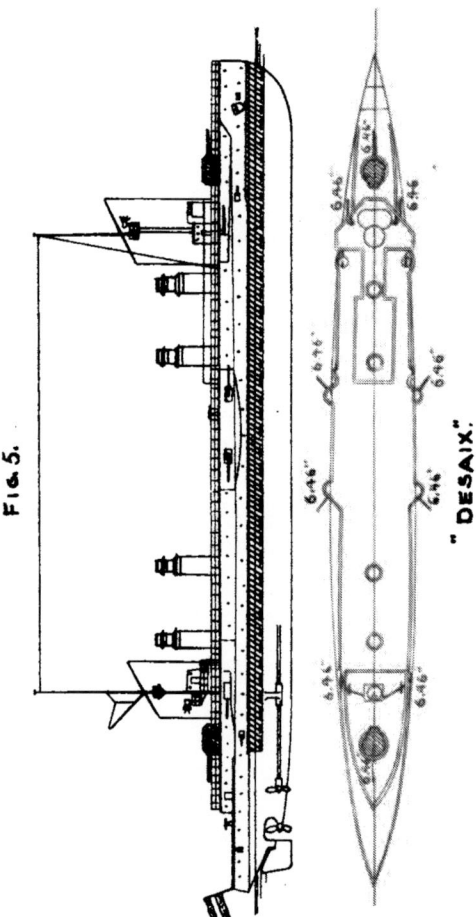

Fig. 5.

"DESAIX."

## FRANCE.

For the year 1897 the ministry submitted to the Chamber a demand for 210,000,000 marks for new constructions, to be completed within eight years. Recognizing the necessity of a strong navy, the people's delegates shortened the period to three years, with the only limitation that the principal sum should be used for the construction of new armored cruisers and about 50,000,000 marks for the remodeling of older ships. For the year 1898 the construction of one battleship (instead of two asked for by the administration), three armored cruisers (instead of one), and eleven torpedo boats was voted, also the necessary funds for completing the ships then under construction. The installment of the heavy guns of the *Suffren* is to be the same as that of the *Jauréguiberry* (four single turrets); but the secondary battery is to be installed in casemates, the same as in the *Brennus*. By the end of the year the following ships will still be in process of construction: Three battleships—*Jéna*, *Suffren*, and *Henry IV*; six armored cruisers of 9,515 tons displacement—*Gueydon*, *Dupetit Thouars*, *Montcalm*, *Le Condé*, *Sully*, and *Gloire*; three armored cruisers of 7,700 tons—*Desaix*, *Kléber*, and *Dupleix*; also the *Jeanne d'Arc*, and finally the station cruisers *Guichen*, *Châteaurenault*, and *Jurien de la Gravière*.

In the discussion of the budget it was particularly pointed out that France had recently built too many different types, as will also appear from the table of French warships given below. The constant changes of dimensions, armor, and distribution of armament prove either that France has hitherto had no definite aim in view, or that former constructions have not proved satisfactory. This may be one of the reasons why the building of warships is so expensive in France. The new minister recognizes these drawbacks. Six armored cruisers, of 9,500 tons displacement, have therefore been ordered, and three of 7,700 tons.

At a first glance it may seem strange that France has asked for only one new battleship, the *Suffren*, but this will be more easily understood if it is remembered that the *Montcalm* class possess all the requirements of battleships, with the exception of the heavy armament. Perhaps, too, France has recognized that her navy, even with the Russian for an ally, is no match for the English navy, and intends in the future, in case of war, to use her battle fleet only for the protection of the coast, but her armored cruisers for the destruction of English commerce, in the face of historical facts and competent opinion.

This intention is given expression in the three protected cruisers. As far as possible these ships are to have the aspect of merchant vessels—straight or overhanging bow and stern, pole masts with gaffs, without fighting tops, etc. The *Guichen* and *Châteaurenault* are to be of the same dimensions as the United States commerce destroyers *Columbia* and *Minneapolis*, but the new French ships are better suited for their purpose. For instance, the coal supply of the *Columbia* is

1,500 tons, while that of the *Guichen* is 2,100 tons. We have already stated that the empire of the sea can be achieved only with battleships in actual battle, and not with cruisers intended to destroy the enemy's commerce.

The following ships made their trial trips last year: Battleships *Masséna, Charlemagne, Gaulois, St. Louis,* and *Bouvet;* armored cruiser *D'Entrecasteaux,* and cruisers *Cassard, Catinat, D'Assas, Lavoisier, Galilée, D'Estrées, Infernet, Protet, La Hire,* and *Dunois.* The *Guichen* commenced her trial trips this year, as provided for in the program. As a general thing all the trial trips have been satisfactory, the *Masséna* being the only ship requiring extensive repairs to the hull. After she had been entirely equipped, it appeared that she was top-heavy, so that at the trial trips the bow buried into the sea considerably; consequently the contract speed was not attained and the steering efficiency was inadequate. The latter defect has since been remedied by enlarging the rudder, and the former by shifting weights and taking on ballast. A few years ago the *Magenta* class and the *Hoche* had also to undergo modifications which cost several million marks, as the stability of the ships proved to be insufficient.

In the following table only the ships under construction have been included:

| Name of ship or class | Henry IV. | Jéna. | Suffren. | Jeanne d'Arc. | Châteaurenault. | Jurien de la Gravière. | Guichen. | Montcalm. | Dupleix. |
|---|---|---|---|---|---|---|---|---|---|
| Number of ships | 1 | 1 | 1 | 1 | 1 | 1 | 1 | 6 | 3 |
| Length | 108 | 122.15 | 125.5 | 145.4 | 135 | 137 | 133 | 138 | 130 |
| Beam | 22 | 20.8 | 21.36 | 19.4 | 17 | 15 | 16.77 | 19.4 | 17.8 |
| Draught (mean)......meters | 7.0 | 8.4 | 7.95 | 8.12 | 6.85 | 6.05 | 7.5 | 7.5 | 7.5 |
| Displacement......tons | 8,948 | 12,052 | 12,728 | 11.270 | 8,018 | 5,686 | 8.277 | 9,517 | 7.700 |
| Speed......knots | 17 | 18 | 18 | 23 | 23 | 23 | 23 | 21 | 21 |
| Horsepower | 11,500 | 15,500 | 16,200 | 28,500 | 23,000 | 17,400 | 23,670 | 19,600 | 17,000 |
| Belt armor......millimeters | (?) | 350 | (?) | 150-50 | | | | 150 | 102-84 |
| Armor of superstructures..do | (?) | 120-80 | (?) | 80-40 | | | | 115 | |
| Deck armor......do | (?) | 65 | (?) | 55 | 35 | 45 | 35 | 50 | 50-22 |
| Armament | 2 27-cm | 2 30.5-cm | 4 30.5-cm | 2 19.4-cm | 2 16.4-cm.in 54 mm. shield. | 8 16-cm | 2 16.4-cm. in 54 mm. shield. | 2 19-cm. in turret, 8 16-cm. in casem. | 10 16-cm. (2 in turret, 8 in 100 mm. casemate). |
| | 7 14-cm | 8 16-cm. in casem. | 10 16-cm. (4 in casem., 6 in turrets). | 8 14-cm. in casem. | 6 13.8-cm. in 54 mm. shield. | 10 4.7-cm | 6 13.8-cm. in 54 mm. shield. | 4 10-cm | 10 4.7-cm |
| | 12 4.7 cm | 8 10-cm. in 54 mm. shields. | 8 10-cm | 10 10-cm | 10 4.7 cm | 6 3.7-cm | 10 4.7-cm | 16 4.7-cm | |
| | 2 sub.l.t | 16 4.7-cm | 20 4.7-cm | 16 4.7-cm | | 2 sub.l.t | | 2 sub.l.t | |
| | | | | 2 sub.l.t | | | | | |
| Coal supply......tons | 1,100 | 800-1,100 | 820-1,150 | 1,400 | 1,400-2,100 | 1,400-1,880 | 1,400-2,100 | 1,020-1,900 | 880-1,200 |

For 1899, two battleships of 14,500 tons with complete armor belt and two dispatch cruisers of 4,000 tons have been granted. In addition to these, the supplementary budget asked for one armored battleship, A 8 (Brest), one armored cruiser of the *Montcalm* type (C 9), two protected cruisers (H 4 and H 5), and six submarine boats (*Narval* type).

Six torpedo-boat destroyers have been given out for construction, namely, *Fouconneau*, *Espignole*, *Pique*, *Epée*, *Framée*, and *Yatagan*, of 50.6 meters length, 5.25 meters beam, 3.02 meters draught, 311 tons displacement, 5,700 horsepower, two deck launching tubes, and a probable speed of 26 knots. There are also under construction or undergoing trials the submarine boats *Gymnote*, *Morse*, and *Gustave Zédé*. These will again be referred to.

The *Amiral Baudin* is being reconstructed, the most important change being the substitution of four 16-centimeter R. F. guns in modern casemates for the central 37-centimeter gun in barbette. The former installation of the heavy guns was similar to that of the German *Brandenburg* class, namely, in three turrets amidships.

The same changes were made in 1897 in the *Formidable*, a sister ship of the *Amiral Baudin*. The boilers have also been changed in these ships. Both have already been placed in commission, but they do not yet have the new casemate armor on board. The reason is said to be that the armor is not yet ready.

The three armored coast-defense vessels, *Indomptable*, *Caïman*, and *Terrible*, are to receive less heavy armament, which will lighten the weight of these ships, for when completely equipped the upper edge of the armor now dips below the surface of the water.

The dispatch boat *Fleurus* is again ready for trial trips. She was launched as early as 1893. The first trial trips were not satisfactory, and the vessel has since been equipped with Niclausse boilers, so that it will be six years from the time of launching before she will be ready for service. Her speed is said to be only 17 knots.

## UNITED STATES.

At the beginning of the year 1898 the following vessels were under construction: Battleships *Kearsarge*, *Kentucky*, *Illinois*, *Alabama*, and *Wisconsin;* gunboat *Princeton*, and sixteen torpedo boats.

None of the larger ships were completed for trial trips in the course of the year. The original naval estimates for 1898 were 128,000,000 marks (35,000,000 marks alone for new constructions), being 10,000,000 marks less than for the preceding year, as it was not the intention to lay down any new large ships. The reason for this was that great difficulties had been encountered in procuring the armor plate for the ships under construction, or that the prices asked for such armor by the manufacturers were too high. But in the discussion of the appropriation bill the laying down of one large battleship was asked for without at first increasing the amount of the estimates. Shortly before the beginning of the Spanish-American war, however, the above figures were increased for the purpose of purchasing additional ships, and at the same time it was recognized that a larger fleet was absolutely necessary, and as a result a bill was passed to lay down during the year three battleships and four armored coast-defense vessels. The battleships were to be of 11,000 tons displacement and of only 16 knots speed. In explanation of the slow speed the Secretary of the Navy made a statement to the effect that a speed of 16 knots is sufficient for United States battleships as long as the ships of other nations do not exceed the rate of 18 knots, and that by making the speed and coal capacity less than for foreign battleships, the United States ships, with the same offensive and defensive qualities, can be built smaller and at less expense.

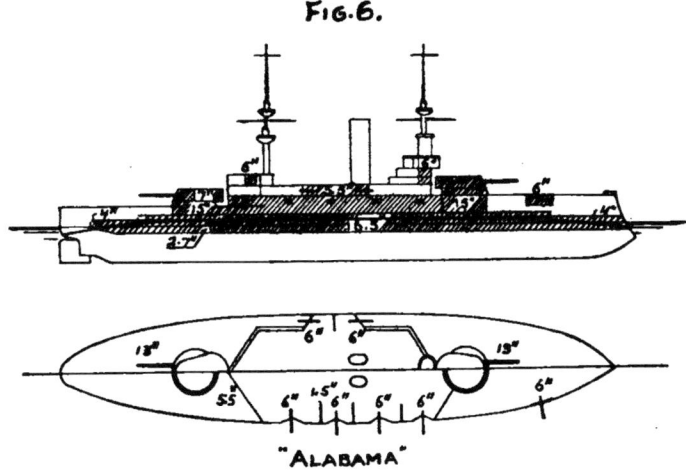

Fig. 6.

"Alabama"

But after the termination of the war, the issue of which was so extremely favorable for the United States, the fleet gained quite a different significance, because the United States, as a result of the war, has entered the ranks of colonial powers and will now require ships of large coal capacity and great speed. The program for the increase of the Navy, for which 220,000,000 marks were voted for new constructions and armament alone, was therefore changed, and now includes three battleships of 13,500 tons, three large armored cruisers of 12,000 tons, three protected cruisers of 6,000 tons,[1] and six unprotected cruisers of 2,500 tons, all of which are to be commenced, if possible, during the present fiscal year, as the funds become available for the Secretary of the Navy on January 1, 1899. Hence there will be under construction in the United States in the course of 1899 eleven battleships, four armored coast-defense vessels, three first-class armored cruisers, six protected and six unprotected cruisers. The three battle-

---

[1] The three protected cruisers of 6,000 tons were not appropriated for.—(O. N. I.)

ships already given out for construction are the *Maine, Missouri,* and *Ohio*.[1] The following sketch shows the distribution of armor and armament.[2]

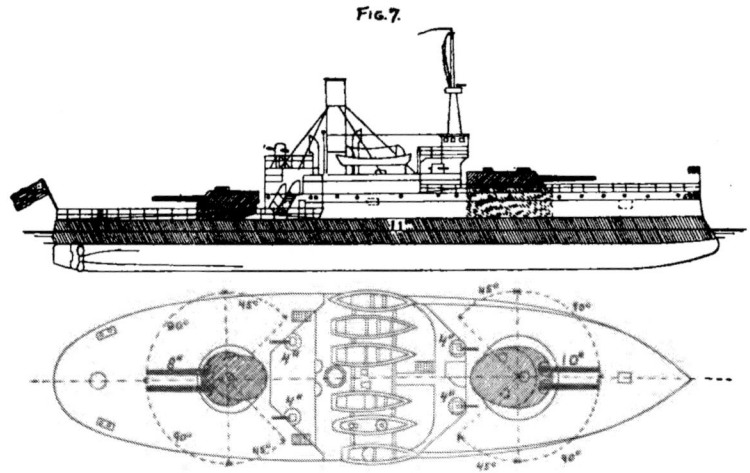

Fig. 7.

The draught is to be 7.75 meters. It is stated that all United States ships are in future to have a wooden skin sheathed with copper.[3]

The four new armored coast-defense vessels, the *Arkansas, Connecticut, Florida,* and *Wyoming,* as shown by the sketch, are built after the pattern of the monitors—peculiar to the United States Navy—except that they have received an additional deck forward, probably for the purpose of making the ships more habitable for the crews rather than of improving their seaworthiness. Building the fore part of the ships 3 meters higher will hardly increase their seaworthiness, and will, moreover, make it impossible to use the bow gun when steaming against an even moderate head sea. The assumption is probably correct that a change in the type of these ships is desirable, if it can still be done, and according to the latest information this appears to be the intention.[4]

It is not easy to understand why the American ships have hitherto been given so little free board, and, independent of this, such narrow quarters for the crews; but the complements of American ships are comparatively small. The crew of the *Alabama,* for instance, consists of only 490 men, while the ships of our *Brandenburg* class, of 1000

---

[1] These ships will be of 12,500 tons displacement and have a speed of 18 knots.—(O. N. I.)

[2] Figure 7 is the plan of a double-turret monitor prepared unofficially for parties who were seeking to procure appropriations for new vessels for the naval militia. It was illustrated in Yachting in the fall of 1897.—(O. N. I.)

[3] The statement that the new ships will have a wooden skin, sheathed with copper, is misleading. The ships will be built of steel, the underwater body sheathed with wood and coppered.—(O. N. I.)

[4] This is an error, as the new monitors will have no additional forward deck, but will be like the original type.—(O. N. I.)

Fig. 8.

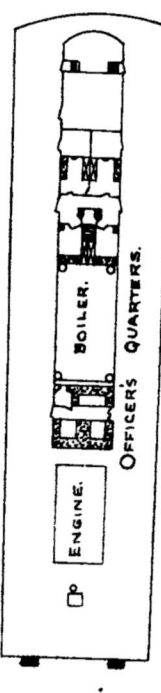
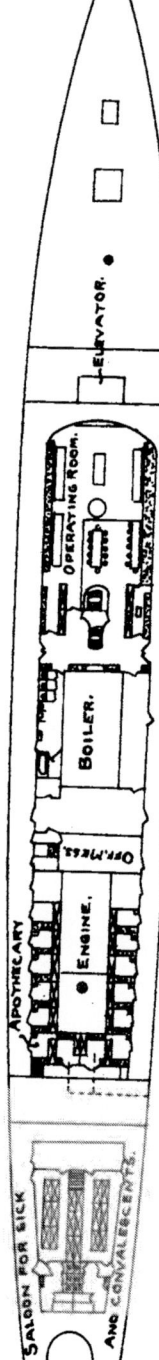
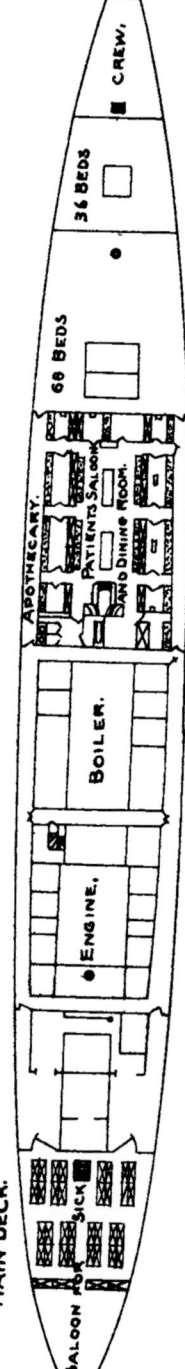

PROMENADE DECK.

UPPER DECK.

MAIN DECK.

U.S. HOSPITAL SHIP "SOLACE".

tons less displacement, have complements of 550 men, and the larger French battleships, *Charlemagne* and *Brennus*, even 696 and 630 men, respectively.

As special items of interest, we will add that in the trial trips of the torpedo boat *Stiletto* liquid fuel was used; and further, that at the breaking out of the war the merchant steamer *Solace* was fitted out as a hospital ship.

The following war ships were purchased direct during the Spanish-American war: Protected cruisers *Albany* and *New Orleans* (formerly *Abreu* and *Amazonas*), and the dynamite cruiser *Buffalo* (formerly *Nictheroy*), with an aggregate displacement of 14,000 tons.

It can not yet be determined which of the ships captured at Santiago can be floated and again made serviceable. This applies also to the auxiliary navy, many vessels of which will probably be sold again.

| Name of type ship | Alabama. | Maine. | Armored ships, Nos. 13-15. | Arkansas. | First-class armored cruisers. | Second-class protected cruisers.[1] | Unprotected cruisers. |
|---|---|---|---|---|---|---|---|
| Number in class | 3 | 3 | 3 | 4 | 3 | 3 | 6 |
| Length......meters.. | 112.6 | 117.6 | | 61 | | | |
| Beam..........do... | 22.6 | 21.9 | | 15.25 | | | |
| Draft (mean)....do... | 7.16 | 7.2 | | 3.8 | | | |
| Displacement..tons.. | 11,525 | 12,300 | 13,500 | 2,500 | 12,000 | 6,000 | 2,500 |
| Speed........knots.. | 16 | 18 | 18 | 13 | 22 | 20 | 16 |
| Horsepower.......... | 10,000 | 16,000 | | 3,500 | | | |
| Belt armor, millimeters | 418-240 | 305 | | 280 | | | |
| | 150 | 139 | | | | | |
| Deck armor, millimeters | 70-101 | 126-70 | | | | | |
| Armament | 4 33-cm. in turret. | 4 33-cm. | 4 30.5-cm. | 2 25.4-cm. | 4 20-cm. | 2 20-cm. | |
| | 14 15-cm. in casemate. | 14 15-cm. (8 in casemate). | 14 15-cm. | 2 20-cm. | 12 15-cm. | 12 12-cm. | |
| | 16 5.7-cm. | 24 R. F. | | 2 10-cm. | | | |
| | | | | 4 7.5-cm. | | | |
| Coal supply, nautical miles | 6,000 | 6,000 | 8,000 | | 10,000 | 12,000 | 13,000 |

[1] Congress did not appropriate for the 6,000-ton cruisers. The batteries and dimensions of the ships authorized this year will probably undergo some changes.—(O. N. I.)

## JAPAN.

This country is evidently about to develop into the greatest commercial and naval power of the East. While in 1896 the annual expense for the navy amounted to only about 20,000,000 marks, the budget for 1897 rose to 147,000,000 marks, and, as far as can now be estimated, it will be very much higher still for 1898.

The naval program contemplates the creation by 1903 of a navy of 67 large ships and 12 torpedo-boat destroyers, with a total displacement of 260,000 tons. The first great addition to the Japanese navy was made at the termination of the war with China, by the capture of

Chinese ships with a total displacement of 15,000 tons. This increased the number of large ships to 43, of a total displacement of 79,000 tons.

By the end of the year 1897 the number of vessels completed or given out for construction was about 55, with a total tonnage of 160,000. By the end of the year 1898 it had reached 63, with a tonnage of 225,000.

According to the new classification made this year, Japan will have completed or under construction by the end of 1898 six first-class battleships: *Fuji, Yashima, Shikishima, Asahi,* and two unnamed; one third-class battleship: *Chen Yuen;* seven first-class cruisers; *Asama, Tokiwa, Yakuma, Azuma,* and three unnamed; ten second-class cruisers: *Naniwa, Takachiho, Itsukushima, Matsushima, Hashidate, Yoshino, Takasago, Kasagi, Chitose,* and one unnamed; six third-class cruisers: *Idzumi, Chiyoda, Akitsushima, Suma, Akashi,* and one unnamed; sixteen third-class coast-defense vessels; two first-class gunboats; fifteen second-class gunboats; four dispatch boats; seven torpedo-boat destroyers; six first-class torpedo boats; four second-class torpedo boats, and twenty-seven third-class torpedo boats.

The ships under construction during the year 1898 are shown in the following table:

| Type | First-class battleships. | | | First-class armored cruisers. | | | | | Second-class cruisers. | | | Third-class cruisers. | | Dispatch boat. |
|---|---|---|---|---|---|---|---|---|---|---|---|---|---|---|
| Name | SHIKISHIMA. | ASAHI. | Unnamed. | AZUMA. | ASAMA. | TOKIWA. | 2 unnamed. | YAKUMA. | Unnamed. | CHITOSE. | Unnamed. | KASAGI. | TAKASAGO. | SUMA. AKASHI. | MIYAKO. |
| Where built | Thames Iron Works. | Thomson. Clydebank | Armstrong. Elswick. | Société des Chantiers. | Armstrong, Elswick. | Elswick. | Armstrong, Elswick. | Vulcan. | Japan. | Union Iron Works. | Cramp, Philadelphia. | Cramp, Philadelphia. | Armstrong, Elswick. | Japan. | Japan. |
| Year of completion | 1899 | 1899 | 1900 | 1900 | 1898 | 1898 | 1899 | 1900 | | 1898 | Same as Chitose. | | | | |
| Length...meters | 122 | 122 | | 136 | 125 | 124 | 124 | 124 | | 100.6 | | 123.4 | 109 | 91 | 96 |
| Beam...do | 23 | 23 | | 18 | 20.4 | 20 | 20 | 20 | | 15.5 | | 14.9 | 14.2 | 12 | 7 |
| Draught (mean) meters | 8.3 | 8.3 | | 7.3 | 7.4 | 7.3 | 7.3 | 7.3 | | 6 | | 5.35 | 5.4 | 4.6 | 4 |
| Displacement tons | 14,850 | 14,850 | 15,140 | 9,436 | 9,750 | 9,750 | 9,906 | 9,800 | 9,600 | 5,700 | | 4,760 | 4,300 | 2,800 | 1,800 |
| Speed...knots | 18 | 18 | | 20 | 21.25 | 21.25 | | 21 | | 21 | | 22.5 | | 20 | 20 |
| I.H.P | 14,500 | 15,000 | | 17,000 | 18,000 | 18,000 | | 15,500 | | 17,000 | | | 15,500 | 8,500 | 6,130 |
| Belt armor, millimeters | 101-228 | Same as Shikishima. | | 160 | 177 | 177 | 177 | 177 | | | | | | | |
| Armor of superstructures, millimeters | 152 | | | 152 | 152 | 152 | 152 | 152 | | | | 45-114 | | | |
| Deck armor, millimeters | 101 | | | 51 | 50 | 50 | 50 | 51 | Same as Azuma. | | | | | | |
| Armament | 4 30.5-cm. 14 15-cm. in casem. 20 7.5-cm. 12 4.7-cm. 1 a.w.l.t. 4 sub.l.t. | | | 4 20 cm. 12 15-cm. 12 7.5-cm. 12 4.7-cm. Sub.l.t. 1 a.w.l.t. | 4 20-cm. 14 15-cm. (10 in casem.) 15-cm. (4 in shields). 19 r.f. | 4 20-cm. 14 15-cm. 12 7.5-cm. 7 4.7-cm. 4 sub.l.t. 1 n.w.l.t. | | | | 4 20-cm. 8 12.7-cm. 12 5.7-cm. 4 3.7-cm. | | 2 20-cm. 10 12-cm. 12 7.5-cm. 12 5.7-cm. 12 3.7-cm. 5 l.t. | 2 20-cm. 15 10-cm. 12 7.5-cm. 6 4.7-cm. | 2 15-cm. 6 12-cm. 12 4.7-cm. | |
| Coal supply, tons | 780 | | | 1,300 | 1,300 | 1,300 | | | | | | 350-1,000 | | | |
| Complement | | | | | | | | | | | | 405 | | | |

It will be seen from the above table that in construction of new material Japan is ahead of all other powers with the exception of England. The four new battleships are probably the most powerful warships of the world. They are almost equal in armament to the largest battleships of the *Majestic* class, which they will probably exceed in speed and horsepower. Moreover, their armor is to extend along the whole water line, while the *Majestic* type has an armor belt for only two-thirds of the ship's length. The dimensions are similar to those of the *Majestic* class. As to the other data given in the table, we will state that the figures relating thereto in different publications do not entirely agree.

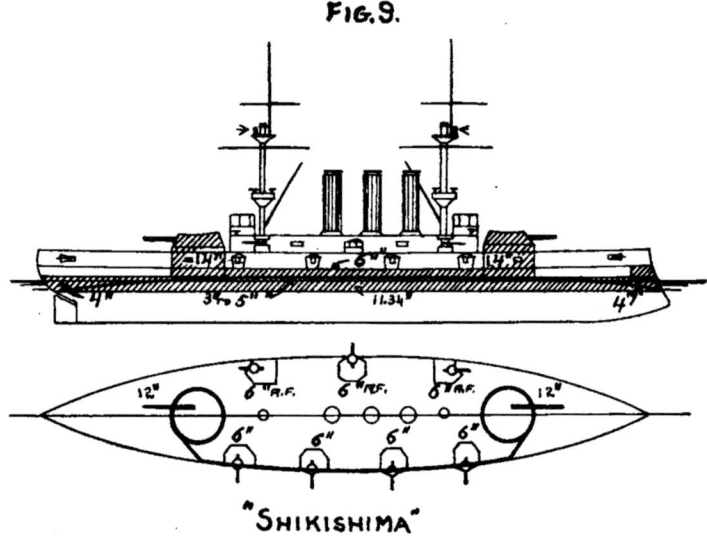

FIG. 9.

"SHIKISHIMA"

It will appear from the foregoing table that uniformity has not been adhered to in the Japanese navy; but if we take into consideration that slight inaccuracies in the figures are not excluded, it becomes probable that the four battleships and seven first-class armored cruisers given out for construction will be uniform among themselves, with only slight immaterial differences, so that they can be united into a squadron. Hence, aside from their other defensive qualities, they will probably, by cooperating with each other, be superior to the ships of any European power that might eventually become their adversaries in Japanese waters with the exception of the new English armored cruisers.

Outside of the cruisers enumerated in the table, it seems that during the last year two more armored cruisers, of 9,000 tons displacement, which were being built in England for Chile, and which the latter country was not able to accept for lack of funds, have been added to the Japanese navy. The same is said to apply to the *Almirante Barroso*, which Brazil has ordered to be built.

Much attention is also being given to the creation of an auxiliary fleet worthy of the war fleet. Japan is acting quite independently in this matter, and has even now under construction two hospital ships, to be used in case of war.

Finally, it is worthy of notice that Japan, besides many small vessels, has undertaken the construction of a first-class armored cruiser in her own yards.

## RUSSIA.

The original naval estimates for the year 1898 were only 120,000,000 marks. As already stated in connection with the English budget, the Czar allowed, last May, 90,000,000 rubles for the increase of the navy.

At the beginning of the year there were under construction battleships *Peresviet* and *Oslabya*, first-class cruiser *Gromoboy*, for the Baltic fleet, and battleships *Tri Sviatitelia* and *Kniaz Potemkin Tavritchesky*; in all, four battleships and one large armored cruiser, a total of about 60,000 tons displacement. By the end of the year there were under construction ships with a total displacement of 180,000 tons, namely, seven first-class battleships, one first-class armored cruiser, eleven second-class armored cruisers, four third-class cruisers and small vessels. Nothing is as yet known as to the armor of the new ships given out for construction. From data obtainable as to prospective speed, it would seem that the *Kniaz Potemkin Tavritchesky*, with 16 knots, is intended for the reenforcement of the Black Sea fleet in case of war, while the other ships appear to be intended in the first place for service abroad. It is noteworthy that the new battleships are again to be equipped with 30.5-centimeter guns, while for the armament of the *Peresviet* the heaviest guns were of 25-centimeter caliber.

The new cruiser *Gromoboy* is to be a sister ship of the *Rossia*, with only slight differences in the armament and other changes made necessary by the progress in construction of torpedo armament. Among the new second-class cruisers, the seven being constructed for a 23-knot speed deserve special attention. As they carry only medium-caliber guns, they appear to be intended as commerce destroyers. Of the four new third-class cruisers the exceptional speed of 25 knots is expected. As they are to receive a comparatively large radius of action (5,000 miles) and excellent armament, the protective deck can not be given much thickness. In order to attain the desired speed the ratio of the length to the breadth is 9.7 to 1. It appears strange that these cruisers are to have six torpedo-launching tubes. Perhaps this is the cause of their existence.

It is further worthy of notice that Russia is building a number of gunboats adapted to enter the shallow waters on the Chinese coast. The dimensions and other data relative to one of these gunboats, the *Gilyak*, have been included in the table below. Russia is also building a 2,500-ton vessel for carrying and laying mines.

The increase of the Russian volunteer fleet is also progressing.

26

| Type. | First-class battleships. | | | First-class armored cruisers. | Second-class armored cruisers. | | | Third-class cruisers. | Gunboat. |
|---|---|---|---|---|---|---|---|---|---|
| Names of ships | Peresviet, Oslabya, Pobieda. | Kniaz Potemkin Tavritchesky. | Retvisan. | Cesarevitch. | 2 unnamed. Gromoboy. | Bayan. | Novik, Bogatyr, Varyag. | 3 unnamed. | Diana, Pallada, Aurora, Askold. | 4 unnamed. | Gilyak. |
| Where built | Petersburg | Nikolaiev. | Cramp, Philadelphia. | Société des Forges et Chantiers. | Sebastopol. Petersburg | Société des Forges et Chantiers. | Vulcan, Cramp, Havre. | Russia. | Petersburg, Germania. | Russia. | Petersburg |
| Length .......meters | 130 | 113.5 | 114 | 118 | 144.2 | 135 | 122 | 122 | 125.8 | 117 | 63.08 |
| Beam .......do | 22 | 22.2 | 22 | 23 | 20.87 | 17.4 | 16.15 | 16.15 | 16.98 | 12.2 | 11.27 |
| Draft (mean) .......do | 7.9 | 8.2 | 7.95 | 7.93 | 7.9 | 6.7 | 6.10 | 6.10 | 6.4 | 4.9 | ...... |
| Displacement .......tons | 12,674 | 12,480 | 12,700 | 13,100 | 12,357 | 7,890 | 6,250 | 6,000 | 6,630 | 3,000 | 963 |
| Speed .......knots | 18 | 16 | 18 | 18 | 19 | 21 | 23 | 23 | 20 | 25 | 12 |
| I.H.P | 14,500 | 10,600 | 15,000 | 16,500 | 14,500 | 16,500 | 20,000 | 18,000 | 11,000 | | 1,000 |
| Belt armor..millimeters | 288 | 400 | 228 | 228 | | 254 | | | | | |
| Armor of superstructures ..... millimeters | | | | | Probably same type as Tri Sviatitelia. | | | | | | |
| Deck armor .......do | | | 101 | 101 | Similar to Rossia. | 76 | | 63 | | | |
| Armament | 4 25-cm. | 4 30.5-cm. | | 4 30.5-cm. | Sub. l. t. | 2 20-cm. | 2 15-cm. | 12 15-cm. | 6 15-cm. | 6 12-cm. | 4 12-cm. |
|  | 11 15-cm. | 8 15-cm. | | 12 15 cm. | | 8 15-cm. | 12 7.5-cm. | 12 7.5-cm. | 6 12-cm. | 6 4.7-cm. | 5 7.5-cm. |
|  | 16 7.6-cm. | 4 12.7-cm. | | 20 7.6-cm. | | 20 7.8-cm. | 6 4.7-cm. | 6 4.7-cm. | 27 R. F. | 6 1. t. | 4 4.7-cm. |
|  | 28 R. F. | 20 R. F. | | 2 6.2-cm. | | 7 4.7-cm. | 2 sub. l. t. | 2 sub. l. t. | | | 2 1. t. |
|  |  | 7 l. t. | | 20 4.7-cm. | | | | | | | |
| Coal supply .......tons | | | | | | | 500 | 500 | | 500 | |

FIG. 10.

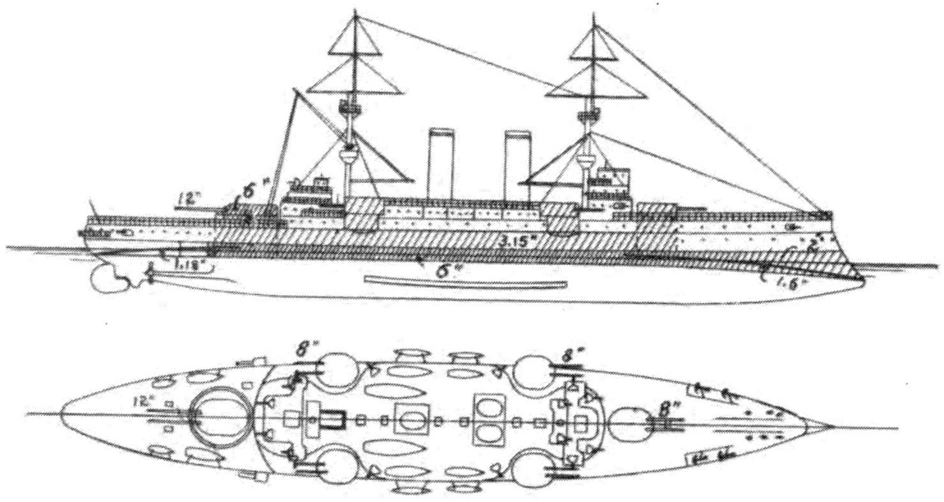

FIRST CLASS BATTLESHIP
"BENEDETTO BRIN".

## ITALY.

During the year 1898 the Italian navy has had to deplore the loss of Minister Brin. He was minister of marine for seven terms, and most of the new battleships of the Italian navy were built by him. In their construction he would often deviate from the course prescribed by other navies and follow out his own ideas.

At the time of the death of Minister Brin the value of the Italian navy amounted to about 800,000,000 marks. Lately the construction of new ships has had to be very much restricted, owing to constant lack of funds. It is probable that it was for this reason that the Italian Government consented to the sale to foreign powers of the ships *Guiseppe Garibaldi* and *Varese*, both built for Italy at private yards. The *Guiseppe Garibaldi* is now being built for the third time. The first went to the Argentine Republic under the name *Garibaldi*, the second was sold to Spain under the name of *Cristobal Colon*, and the *Guiseppe Garibaldi* No. 3, now under construction, is said to have also been sold to the Argentine Republic. The *Varese*, Nos. 1 and 2, were also sold to the Argentine Republic under the names of *General San Martino* and *General Belgrano*.

Besides the above, there were in process of construction or equipment during the past year the battleships *Ammiraglio di St. Bon* and *Emanuele Filiberto*, and the small cruisers *Puglia, Agordat*, and *Coatit*. This shows very little activity, considering the size of the Italian navy. But, as the joint manœuvres of the army and navy during the previous year have demonstrated that the coasts, without the existence of a strong fleet, are exposed to easy hostile landings, it was decided to begin in 1898 the construction of three new battleships, for which Minister Brin drew the plans. These are the *Benedetto Brin, Ammiraglio Bacchia,* and *Margherita*. They are to be of the following dimensions: Length, 126 meters; beam, 23.84 meters; draught, 8.25 meters; displacement, 12,765 tons. The armor belt extends from the forward to the after conning tower. Its thickness of 15 centimeters gradually decreases to 50 millimeters forward. The protective deck, 40 to 80 millimeters thick, extends over the whole length of the ship. The I. H. P. is 18,000; the speed 20 knots, and the coal bunkers are adapted to hold from 1,000 to 2,000 tons. The installation of the armament is shown in the sketch.

There are two 30.5-centimeter, ten 20-centimeter, sixteen 7.6-centimeter, and eight 4.7-centimeter guns, and four torpedo-launching tubes. The installation of the two 30.5-centimeter guns aft is peculiar. These three new battleships may be designated as a combination of an armored cruiser and a battleship.

The *Duilio* has been reconstructed, following the modifications of the *Dandolo*, which was previously completed.

During the past year Italy commenced the creation of an auxiliary fleet, into which merchant steamers of over 7,000 tons displacement and 18 knots speed may be received. Contracts for seven such ships have already been made.

## GERMANY.

Germany's young navy suffered a severe loss last year through the death of the former chief constructor, Prof. Alfred Diedrich, privy councillor of the Admiralty, who, since 1879, had been chief of the bureau of construction, and in this capacity had superintended the plans of all new ships.

The program of naval constructions for Germany was determined by the law of April 10, 1898, for the next six years. According to this law, the budget for nonrecurrent expenses is not to exceed an average of 68,000,000 marks; and for continuous expenses an increase of 4,900,000 marks over previous years was granted. Besides the ships under construction April 1, 1898, the following are to be built: Seven battleships, two large and seven small cruisers. The following table will show the dimensions of the ships under construction during the year 1898:

| Names of ships or class | Battle ships A and B, Ersatz König Wilhelm, Kaiser Friedrich III, Kaiser Wilhelm II. | First-class armored cruiser Fürst Bismarck. | Freya, Hertha, Hansa, Vineta, Viktoria Louise. | Large cruiser A. | Gazelle, small cruisers A and B. | Wolf, Habicht, Iltis, Jaguar. |
|---|---|---|---|---|---|---|
| Length .............meters.. | 115 | 120 | 115 | 120 | 100 | 62 |
| Beam.................do.... | 20.4 | 20.4 | 17.4 | 19.6 | 11.8 | 9.1 |
| Draught (mean)......do.... | 7.3 | 7.9 | 6.23 | 7.1 | 4.85 | 3.25 |
| Displacement ........tons.. | 11,081 | 10,650 | 5,628 | 8,860 | 2,645 | 895 |
| Speed ...............knots . | 18 | 18.75 | 19.5 | 20.25 | 19.5 | 13.5 |
| I. H. P.................... | 13,000 | 13,500 | 10,000 | 15,000 | 6,000 (B 7,000, A 8,000). | 1,300 |
| Belt armor....millimeters.. | 300–150 | 200–100 | ............ | 100 | ............ | ............ |
| Armor of superstructures, millimeters. | Turret 150 | Turret 100 | Turret 100 | 100 | ............ | ............ |
| Deck armor...millimeters.. | 75–65 | 50–30 | ............ | 50 | 50–20 | ............ |
| Armament ................ | 4 24-cm. | 4 24-cm. | 2 21-cm. | 2 24-cm. | 10 15-cm. | 4 8.8-cm. |
|  | 12 15-cm. in casem. | 6 15-cm. in casem. | 4 15-cm. in casem. | 10 15-cm. | 14 3.7-cm. | 6 3.7-cm. |
|  | 6 15-cm. in turret. | 6 15-cm. in turret. | 4 15-cm. in turret. | 10 8.8-cm. | 2 a. w. l. t. |  |
|  | 12 8.8-cm. | 10 8.8-cm. | 10 8.8-cm. | 10 3.7-cm. | 1 sub. l. t. |  |
|  | 12 3.7-cm. | 10 3.7-cm. | 10 3.7-cm. | Mach. guns |  |  |
|  | 1 a. w. l. t. | 5 sub. l. t. | 2 sub. l. t. | 3 sub. l. t. |  |  |
|  | 5 sub. l. t. | 1 a. w. l. t. | 1 a. w. l. t. | 1 a. w. l. t. |  |  |
| Coal supply .........tons.. | 650, and 229 tar oil. | 1,000, and 100 tar oil. | 500–900 | 950–1,300 | 500–580 (cr. A 300–380). | 120–160 |
| Complement................ | 642 | 568 | 447 | ............ | 211, 244, 250 | 121 |

At the beginning of the year 1898 there were under construction three battleships, six large cruisers, and two gunboats, the plans of which were published in the Marine-Rundschau last year.

The following ships were given out for construction in the course of the year: Battleships "A" and "B," large cruiser "A," small cruisers "A" and "B," and gunboats *Ersatz Habicht* and *Ersatz Wolf*.

The total displacement of the ships under construction was about 115,000 tons. Special value is attached to obtaining as much uniformity as possible in the same class, so that the ships can be united into squadrons. Thus, all the ships of the *Sachsen*, *Brandenburg*, and *Hertha* class, respectively, are uniform. The battleships "A" and "B" are to be built so that they can be used in connection with the *Kaiser Friedrich III* class.

In the course of the year the *Kaiser Friedrich III*, *Hertha*, *Viktoria Louise*, *Freya*, and *Vineta* were completed, and all of them, as far as appears from the trial trips hitherto made, come up to contract requirements. Extensive modifications have been made in the *Sachsen* class. The *Baden* and *Bayern* are completed, and have already made their trial trips, while the *Württemberg* and *Sachsen* are still in process of reconstruction. The *Kurfürst Friedrich Wilhelm* and *Brandenburg*, of the *Brandenburg* class, have been equipped for the use of liquid fuel (tar oil). Thirty-seven millimeter machine guns have been installed on board all four ships of the *Brandenburg* class.

## AUSTRIA HUNGARY.

The Austrian navy, whose only mission is the defense of a short strip of coast, has not made any special efforts this year.

The two coast defense vessels *Wien* and *Budapest*, of 5,500 tons displacement, and torpedo cruisers *Zenta* and "B" have been completed. Ram cruiser "D" and the *Kaiser Karl VI*, of the *Maria Theresa* type, are almost completed. The turret armor of the latter ship is of 220 millimeters thickness. The armament consists of two 24-centimeter guns in turret, and ten 15-centimeter guns in modern casemates. Displacement, 6,250 tons. Speed, 20 knots.

It is stated that Austria, following the example of other powers, also intends to lay down a definite building programme for the next ten years, which will require 90,000,000 marks in excess of the former budget.

|  | As now existing. | As required. |
|---|---|---|
| Battleships of 6,000–9,000 tons | 11, of which 5 are modern. | 15 |
| Second-class cruisers of 4,000–7,000 tons | 3 ram cruisers. | 7 |
| Third-class cruisers of 1,500–2,500 tons |  | 7 |
| Torpedo dispatch boats | 8 | 15 |

At the trial trips of the three coast-defense vessels, *Monarch*, *Wien*, and *Budapest*, it appeared that they took over a great deal of water on the forward deck even in smooth water. This defect will render it very difficult to aim the forward guns while steaming at full speed.

## SPAIN.

In anticipation of difficulties with America, Spain made great efforts in 1898 and modernized some of her older ships, like the *Numancia*, *Vitoria*, and *Pelayo;* but the fatal catastrophe could not be averted. So much has been written about the war that we will here only briefly refer to its results as far as they affect the status of the Spanish fleet. Spain lost in all forty-five vessels, with a total displacement of 48,042 tons, among them twelve cruisers with a total displacement of 42,974 tons. The vessels lost at Cavite were the *Isla de Cuba, Reina Cristina, Castilla, Don Antonio de Ulloa, Don Juan de Austria, Velasco, El Cano, General Lezo*, and *Marqués del Duero;* at Santiago, the *Oquendo, Infanta María Teresa, Vizcaya,* and *Cristobal Colon*.[1] Of all these vessels, the four last named were the only ones that possessed real fighting efficiency.

## NORWAY.

Two double-turreted armor clads, the *Harald Haarfagre* and *Tordenskjold*, built in England, were launched in 1897. It is now stated that the Norwegian navy is to be further increased. It is true that for the current year only about 4,000,000 marks have been voted for new constructions, but an additional demand has been made for the navy to the amount of 18,000,000 marks. Of this sum, 11,000,000 marks are to be used in the construction of three new armored ships. Judging from the price, these will be similar to the above-mentioned coast-defense armor clads.

## SWEDEN.

The Swedish navy has six second-class battleships, five of which are ready for war. The latest ships are the *Oden, Thor,* and *Njord,* of 3,400 tons displacement and the same dimensions as the two Norwegian ships above mentioned, but of somewhat higher speed. On other vessels work is going on for the purpose of modernizing them and changing the armament.

## OTHER NAVIES.

We will not speak at length of the navies of other European countries, like Turkey, Roumania, Portugal, Denmark, and Holland, because they have only a few small vessels under construction.

Of other nations outside of Europe, China has two cruisers under construction at Armstrong's, the *Hai Tsin* and the *Hai Tschi*, of 4,300

---

[1] This statement is incomplete. It omits a number of Spanish naval vessels captured or destroyed at the two places named.—(O. N. I.)

Fig. 11.—SCHICHAU TORPEDO-BOAT DESTROYER (35.2 KNOTS).

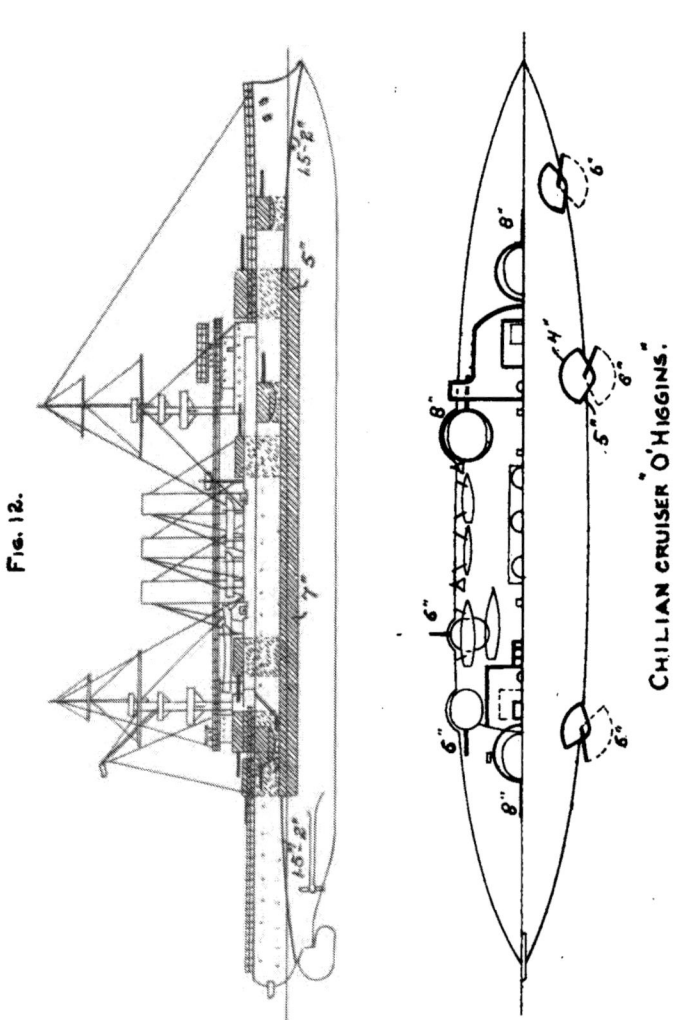

Fig. 12.

Chilian Cruiser "O'Higgins."

Fig. 13.

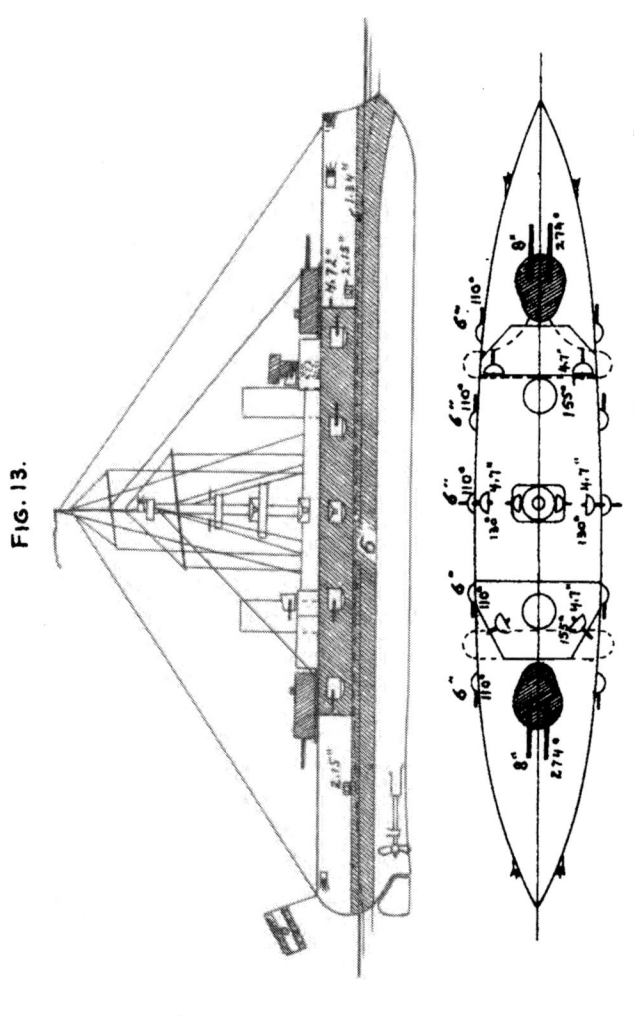

ARGENTINE ARMORED CRUISER "GENERAL SAN MARTINO"

tons displacement, and the *Hai Tschen*, of 2,950 tons, at the Vulcan Works, Stettin, where two protected cruisers of the same size are also being built. Several torpedo boats of about 1,000 tons displacement have also been ordered.

The torpedo boat destroyers built by Schichau at Elbing, and already delivered to China, deserve special notice, as they have a speed of over 35 knots, and are therefore the fastest ships of the world.

We will add a few noteworthy facts in connection with the South American countries—Chile, Argentine Republic, and Brazil.

Chile had the *General O'Higgins* built, a modern armored cruiser, of 8,500 tons displacement and a speed of 21.25 knots. The sketch shows the peculiar installation of her guns.

The Argentine Republic, as mentioned above, purchased the *General San Martino* and *General Belgrano*, originally built for the Italian navy, both modern and fast armored cruisers of 6,840 tons. Argentina has now three of these cruisers, which form the nucleus of her fleet.

Brazil had under construction in France in 1898 two armored coast-defense vessels, the *Maresciallo Deodoro* and the *Maresciallo Floriana*, of 3,100 tons displacement, and at the Germania Works at Kiel, a torpedo cruiser, the *Tamayo*, of 1,000 tons displacement and 23 knots speed; also a protected cruiser of 3,000 tons.

o

Printed by Libri Plureos GmbH in Hamburg, Germany